Wonders
of Iceland

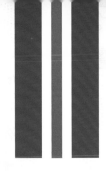

Wonders
of Iceland

A Survey of its History
and Geography, along with some
Useful Information for Travellers

JPV ÚTGÁFA

THE WIDE WORLD OF ICELAND

What makes Iceland such an amazing place, physically and intellectually? Is it the extraordinary quality of light which sharpens the farthest horizons? Is it the unearthly gleam of distant glaciers merging with the heavens themselves? Is it the eternal sunshine locked into rhyolite mountains which glow even on the dullest day? Is it the jets of boiling steam which punctuate the most innocent of landscapes with their plumes? Is it the black volcanic sands and lava which cover huge reaches with a sombre shroud?

It is all of these – and much, much more. The wonders of Iceland lie in its endless diversity and contrast: the whole spectrum is here, from profound tranquillity to nature's wildest forces, from intense solitude to companionable closeness. It is a unique world, different from others in character and appearance.

What also makes Iceland so distinctive is the way the land is so much a part of the people – just as much as the people are a part of the land. The chief heritage of Iceland is its treasury of medieval literature, deep-rooted in the living landscape. It has given Icelanders a special sense of identity, of belonging. This national literature, of edda and saga, of history and folktale, is widely read to this day. But it is not only the books which are read; Icelanders read the landscape itself. The landscape utters history in every rock, in every moor, in every mountain. Every vista tells a tale, every place and every place-name enshrines a story or a legend.

There is also a parallel world in Iceland, an otherworld which has held the imagination since the beginning of time. Throughout the centuries people in Iceland liked to believe that they shared their land with other peoples, 'hidden folk' (huldu-fólk), who inhabited rocks and crags, elvish people essentially like humans but on a different plane, normally invisible but capable of showing themselves. The mountains were the homes of giant trolls who would be turned to stone if they were caught by the rays of the rising sun, and the landscape is littered with the petrified relics of these unfortunate creatures. Iceland sets the imagination alight.

Travelling in Iceland is a journey of exploration: of geology,

of history, of literature, of fantasy, of the story of creation itself. This book is a *vade mecum* for that voyage.

More people than ever before are discovering Iceland for themselves today, each in his or her way, finding new experiences, new aspects of the natural environment. Iceland's untamed nature has always been a magnet for visitors, just as much as the purity of its ancient culture. Today it is the 'new' culture in all its creative manifestations which draws the discriminating seeker: pop music and up-to-date lifestyles, along with the classical arts of music and painting and theatre and literature. And one of the most satisfying aspects of the cultural resurgence of the present is its continuity with the past. The age-old literature has been reborn with renewed vigour; the same inspired need to express identity and experience in the Icelandic language prevails now as it did a thousand years ago.

Discovery is a continuous process in Iceland, even for those who have lived here all their lives, because Iceland is never the same place for two days in a row. In this vast northern arena where all winds and weathers meet, the light and the colours and the look of the land change not only from season to season but also from instant to instant. Beneath our feet is the youngest inhabited landmass in Europe, a living geological laboratory constantly experimenting with the landscape; the land is taking shape before our very eyes, something new is constantly being created.

And yet it always remains essentially the same: timeless but of our time, newly-sprung but eternal, a world apart but very much of this world.

Vigdís Finnbogadóttir,
former president of Iceland

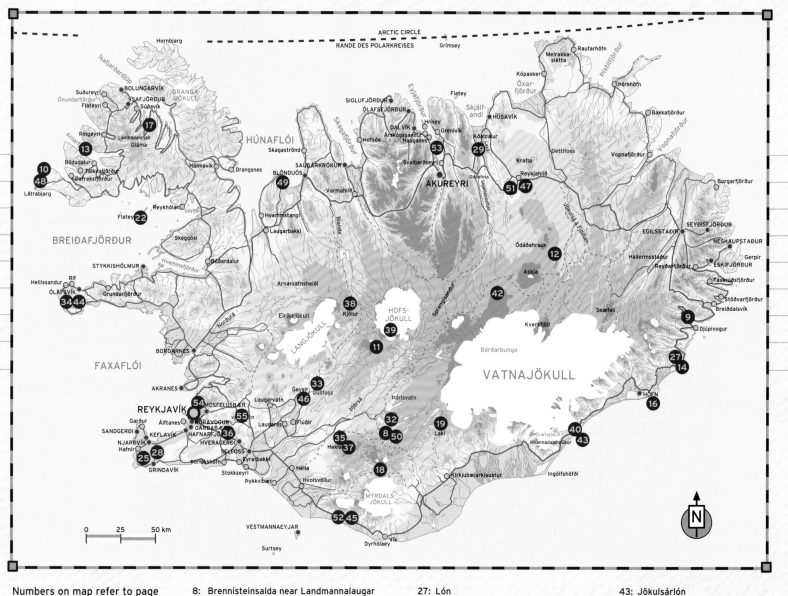

Numbers on map refer to page numbers with photographs.

8: Brennisteinsalda near Landmannalaugar
9: Berufjörður
10: Breiðavík
11: Kerlingarfjöll
12: Herðubreið
13: Hvestudalur in Arnarfjörður
14: Eystrahorn in Lón
16: Stokksnes
17: Skötufjörður
18: North of Mýrdalsjökull
19: Lakagígar
22: Flatey in Breiðafjörður
25: Reykjanes

27: Lón
28: The Blue Lagoon
29: Aðaldalur
32: Veiðivötn
33: Gullfoss
34: Snæfellsjökull
35: Hekla
36: Hellisheiði
37: Hekla
38: Hveravellir
39: Hofsjökull
40: Jökulsárlón
42: North of Vatnajökull

43: Jökulsárlón
44: Snæfellsjökull
45: Skógafoss
46: Geysir in Haukadalur
47: Hverarönd
48: Látravík
49: Hvítserkur
50: Jökulgil near Landmannalaugar
51: Höfði by Lake Mývatn
52: Drangshlíðarfjall
53: Eyjafjörður
54: Kollafjörður
55: Lake Þingvallavatn

CONTENTS

FOREWORD	5
PHOTOGRAPHS	8
HISTORICAL SURVEY	56
THE COUNTRY	58
THE PEOPLE	59
USEFUL INFORMATION	62
TOURIST INFORMATION CENTRES	63
CREDITS	64

Brennisteinsalda near Landmannalaugar

Berufjörður

Breiðavík

At Kerlingarfjöll

Herðubreið

Hvestudalur in Arnarfjörður

Eystrahorn in Lón

Stokksnes

Waterfall in Skötufjörður

North of Mýrdalsjökull

At Lakagígar

Bonfire on New Year's Eve

New Year's Eve in Reykjavík

Flatey in Breiðafjörður

Reykjavík City Hall

"The Pearl" in Reykjavík

Geothermal area on Reykjanes

Sunset in Reykjavík

Bathing in the Blue Lagoon

Rolls of hay in Aðaldalur

Gyrfalcon

Puffins

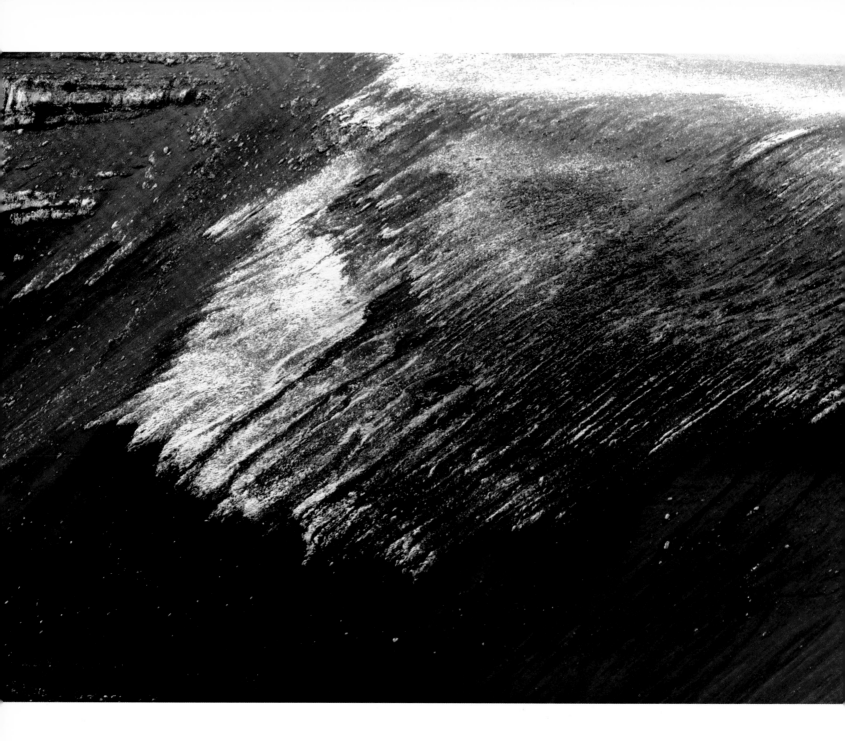

At Veiðivötn

Northern lights above Gullfoss

On top of Snæfellsjökull

Eruption of Hekla in 1991

Crater on Hellisheiði

Eruption of Hekla in 1991

At Hveravellir

Ice climbing on Hofsjökull

Arctic Terns at Jökulsárlón

Öskjuhlíð in Reykjavík

North of Vatnajökull

Jökulsárlón

On top of Snæfellsjökull

Skógafoss in winter

The Great Geysir

Geothermal area at Hverarönd

Látravík

Hvítserkur

Jökulgil near Landmannalaugar

Höfði by Lake Mývatn

Drangshlíðarfjall

Winter in Eyjafjörður

Eroded rocks in Kollafjörður

Lake Þingvallavatn

HISTORICAL SURVEY

MAIN DATES

circa 400 B.C. • The Greek explorer Pytheas describes a land which lies six sailing days north of the British Isles. He calls this land Ultima Thule.

circa 870 • A Swede named Garðar Svavarsson spends the winter on the bay of Skjálfandi in the north of Iceland, where the town of Húsavík is today. He gives the name Garðarshólmi to the land. A Norwegian named Flóki Vilgerðarson makes an unsuccessful attempt at settlement: he establishes himself for the winter at Vatnsfjörður on the northern side of Breiðafjörður, but pack ice drifts up and Flóki's household perishes in the ravages of winter. Flóki himself makes a narrow escape, and before he sails away he gives the land the name which it has borne to this day, Iceland.

874 • Ingólfur Arnarson arrives from Norway and settles in the area of the bay of Faxaflói. He was probably the first man to settle permanently in Iceland, at a place he called Reykjavík – which today is the capital of Iceland. Recently an ancient dwelling-house was excavated in the centre of Reykjavík and dated by experts to the end of the ninth century. Iceland seems to have been fully settled within five decades. It is the last country in Europe to be settled by humans, and no other country in Europe has comparable written records about its origin. The chief record is *Landnámabók* (Book of Settlements), written in the twelfth century. It testifies that most of the settlers came from Norway, some by way of Norse colonies in the British Isles. Old sources like *Landnámabók* and *Íslendingabók* (Book of Icelanders) also tell of Irish hermits who were living in Iceland when the Norsemen came to settle and of how they departed because they refused to associate with heathens. The chief initiative for the settlement came from prosperous farmers and chieftains in Norway who were at odds with the Norwegian king and did not want to be subject to his authority. It is thought that there were between sixty and eighty thousand inhabitants in Iceland at the close of the settlement period. At first

A page from the old manuscript Flateyjarbók (14th century).

there was no centrally organized state or kingdom, but in some districts men gathered at local assemblies in the spring and autumn to deliberate their common affairs.

930–1030 • This period has been called the "Saga Age", because this is when most of the events narrated in the so-called Sagas of Icelanders took place. The establishment of the Alþing (National Assembly) in 930 marks the beginning of this period. From this date, and continuing until 1798, an annual gathering of people from all over the country was held at Þingvellir (Assembly Plains). The Alþing was convened in the tenth week of the summer (in late June) and lasted for two weeks. Its function was to make laws and to render judgments, as well as to make important decisions on matters of common interest. In the Sagas of Icelanders and other old texts Þingvellir is often mentioned as the site of great events.

circa 980 • Eirik the Red initiates the settlement of Greenland by Norsemen.

1000 • The Alþing pronounces Christianity the official religion of Iceland. The conversion to Christianity came peacefully. A compromise was made allowing heathens to continue their sacrificial offerings in private and to continue eating horse-flesh. Also in this year, Leif the Lucky, the son of Eirik the Red, made his way to the east coast of North America.

1056 • An episcopal see is established at Skálholt. The first bishop is Ísleifur Gissurarson, from one of the most powerful chieftain families in Iceland.

1096 • Tithing becomes law in Iceland. The tithe was in fact a property tax levied to support the church. The chieftains profited from this levy, since they owned the church properties and since those in clerical orders were in their service.

1104 • The first eruption of the volcano Hekla after the settlement. An inhabited area in Þjórsárdalur in the south of Iceland is enveloped in pumice and rendered uninhabitable forever. Old farms and a cemetery in this valley were excavated by archaeologists in the 1930s. The remains of the farm at Stöng were magnificently preserved and give us an insight into the construction and arrangement of houses.

1106 • An episcopal see for the north of Iceland is established at Hólar in Hjaltadalur. The first bishop of Hólar is Jón Ögmundsson, who devotes himself to removing the last remnants of heathen belief. He succeeds in eliminating the old names for weekdays, some of which had been based on the heathen gods: Týr (Tuesday), Óðinn (Wednesday), Þór (Thursday) and Freyr (Friday). In the other Germanic languages the old heathen names for the days of the week have remained in place.

1117–1118 • The laws are written down for the first time in Iceland.

circa 1130 • Ari Þorgilsson the Learned composes *Íslendingabók* (Book of Icelanders). This, the first historical text to be written in Icelandic, covers the settlement, the establishment of the Alþing, the conversion to Christianity, the discovery of Greenland and much more.

1150–1200 • The writing down of sagas begins in the monasteries of Iceland. At first the emphasis is placed on the history of the Norwegian kings.

1220–1264 • This period is often called the "Age of the Sturlungs", with reference to one of the most influential chieftain families of this time. Internal dissension and a struggle for power among the leading families characterize this period, at the end of which the Icelanders became subjects of the Norwegian king. This marks the end of the so-called Commonwealth Period, which had lasted for four hundred years.

1241 • Snorri Sturluson, one of the most powerful chieftains in Iceland, is slain at the bidding of Hákon the Old, king of Norway.

1262 • The Icelanders submit to the Norwegian king by signing the *Gamli sáttmáli* (Old Covenant). King Hákon the Old takes advantage of the dissension among Icelandic chieftains in bringing the country under his control. The Icelandic merchant fleet falls into decay and the country becomes dependent on Norway for trade and supplies. Under the terms of the Old Covenant the Norwegian king was to assure that foreign goods reached Iceland. As it turned out, this pledge was sometimes broken in times of difficulty, such as when the Icelandic ports were blocked by pack ice.

1397 • With the forming of the Union of Kalmar, Iceland, together with Norway, becomes a part of the Danish empire.

1402–1404 • The Black Death reaches Iceland, killing approximately one-third of the population.

1490 • England receives permission from the Danish king to fish off the coast of Iceland.

1540–1550 • The Reformation reaches Scandinavia. The King of Denmark appropriates the churches and monasteries, and the economic situation of Iceland suffers greatly as church revenues pass from Iceland into the treasury of the Danish crown. The New Testament is printed in Icelandic for the first time in 1540.

1550 • Jón Arason, the last Catholic bishop in Iceland, is killed at Skálholt, after putting up a stiff resistance to the Reformers.

1584 • The Bible in its entirety is printed for the first time in Icelandic translation, at the instigation of Guðbrandur Þorláksson, bishop of Hólar.

1602 • The beginning of the Danish "monopoly trade". The Danish king gives Danish merchants exclusive rights to carry on trade in Iceland. The country is divided into commercial districts, and Icelanders are required to carry on trade exclusively with the merchant in their district. Harsh punishment is dealt to offenders.

1662 • The most important leaders of the country are summoned to a meeting in Kópavogur where they are required to

Commemorating the eleven-hundreth anniversary of the settlement of Iceland at Þingvellir in 1974.

The Icelandic flag.

Eruption on Westman Islands in 1973.

swear an oath of allegiance to Frederik III, king of Denmark, recognizing him as sole ruler of the country.

1703 • The first general census in Iceland.

1709–1712 • A smallpox epidemic kills approximately one-third of the inhabitants of Iceland.

1783–1785 • One of the most powerful eruptions in recorded history occurs at the Laki craters along a 30 kilometre stretch in the south of Iceland. A large proportion of the livestock dies, resulting in a devastating famine. It is reckoned that as many as ten thousand people died of starvation, one fourth of the inhabitants. This event is referred to as the "Mist Famine" on account of the polluted haze which hung in the air for a long time afterwards, even drifting to other countries.

1787 • The monopoly trade is suspended and all subjects of the king of Denmark are permitted to trade freely.

1799 • The Alþing is discontinued.

1801 • The High Court is established in Reykjavík.

1809 • Jörgen Jörgensen, a Danish adventurer, lands in Reykjavík, declares himself monarch and holds power for a period of two months.

1818 • Founding of the National Library.

1843 • The Alþing is revived as an advisory assembly. The struggle for Icelandic independence starts, under the leadership of Jón Sigurðsson.

1848 • The first Icelandic daily newspaper begins circulation.

1854 • Iceland receives unrestricted freedom to carry on trade.

1863 • A museum of antiquities is established, the predecessor of the National Museum of Iceland.

1874 • A great celebration is held at Þingvellir commemorating the millennium of the settlement of Iceland. King Christian IX visits Iceland, the first Danish king to do so, and presents the Icelanders with a constitution.

1904 • Iceland receives home rule. Hannes Hafstein becomes the first Icelandic prime minister.

1906 • An underwater telephone cable is laid between Scotland and Iceland.

1911 • Founding of the University of Iceland.

1915 • Iceland receives its own flag.

1918 • Iceland becomes an independent and sovereign state with ties to the Danish crown. The Spanish Influenza rages in Reykjavík. Volcanic eruption at Katla. Devastating frost in the first part of the year, which is still referred to as "The Big Freeze".

1920 • Founding of the Supreme Court.

1930 • Celebration of the millennium of the Alþing.

1940 • Iceland is occupied by British forces in the Second World War. Its situation in the middle of the Atlantic Ocean gives Iceland great strategic importance. One year later the British troops are replaced by Americans.

1944 • The union with Denmark is broken. The founding of the Republic of Iceland is celebrated at Þingvellir.

1946 • Iceland joins the United Nations.

1949 • Iceland takes part in the founding of the North Atlantic Treaty Organization.

1950 • Iceland joins the Council of Europe. The National Theatre is inaugurated and the Icelandic Symphony Orchestra is founded.

1952 • Iceland extends its territorial waters to four nautical miles. Iceland joins the Nordic Council.

1955 • Halldór Laxness is awarded the Nobel Prize for Literature.

1958 • The territorial waters are extended to twelve nautical miles. This leads to the first "Cod War" with the British, who send warships to the Icelandic fishing grounds to protect their fishing fleet. This international dispute ends three years later, when the British recognize the new fisheries jurisdiction.

1963–1967 • A new island comes into existence in a large underwater eruption to the south of Iceland; it receives the name Surtsey.

1964 • Iceland enters the European Free Trade Association.

1966 • The first television station in Iceland begins operations.

1967 • Herring catches fail. The decline in the herring stock is a serious blow to the Icelandic economy.

1971 • Denmark hands over to Iceland the first of the old manuscripts which had been preserved in Danish collections. These manuscripts had long been regarded as the most precious national treasure of Iceland.

1972 • Iceland extends its territorial waters to fifty nautical miles. A new "Cod War" breaks out: the British send a fleet of warships to Icelandic waters, but eventually the two countries agree on the extended limits.

1973 • A volcanic eruption on Heimaey, the only settled island in the Westman group of islands off the southern coast of Iceland. All the inhabitants, around 5,300, are swiftly transported off the island. The eruption lasts for nearly half a year, after which many of the inhabitants return home. The presidents of the United States and France, Richard Nixon and George Pompidou, meet in Reykjavík.

1974 • Ceremonies in commemoration of the eleven-hundredth anniversary of the settlement of Iceland. The highway encircling the whole island is completed.

1975 • Iceland once again extends its territorial waters, this time to two hundred nautical miles. This leads to a bitter dispute with Great Britain. An agreement is reached after two years when the British recognize the new limits; the third "Cod War" ends in victory for Iceland.

1980 • Vigdís Finnbogadóttir is elected president of the Republic, becoming the first woman in the world to be chosen as head of state in an open election.

1983 • The first women's political party in Iceland is founded.

1986 • Ceremonies commemorating the two-hundredth anniversary of Reykjavík as a licensed trading centre. Ronald Reagan and Mikail Gorbachev, the leaders of the United States and the Soviet Union, meet in Reykjavík. Their meeting marks a turning point in the Cold War which had existed between the two countries for years.

1989 • The government places severe fishing restrictions on cod, which had always been the fish most caught by Icelanders. Pope John Paul comes to Iceland, the first papal visit to the country. Whaling is banned in Icelandic waters.

1994 • Ceremonies commemorating the fiftieth anniversary of the Republic.

2000 • Ceremonies commemorating the millennium of the conversion to Christianity in Iceland.

THE COUNTRY

Geographical Situation

Iceland is an island in the northern Atlantic Ocean, lying at the juncture of tectonic plates reaching to the arctic circle and lying midway between the continents of Europe and North America. The island is a part of the great undersea ridge which extends the entire length of the Atlantic Ocean from north to south.

Geology

In Iceland, the two continents are drifting apart from each other at an average of two centimetres a year. At the place where the tectonic plates meet, an active volcanic range stretches across the country. Magma from the bowels of the earth beneath Iceland is constantly pushing up towards the surface, causing continuous eruptions. Because of this, the landscape is constantly changing; Iceland is considered quite young in geological terms.

The erosive power of the sea, not to mention waterfalls, glaciers and winds, contributes to the formation of the landscape. Sources from various times testify to undersea eruptions off the coast of Iceland. Islands and steep rock formations have managed now and then to protrude from the sea in spite of powerful ocean currents which wear them away and often break them down as fast as they are formed. The Westman Islands, a cluster of islands off the southern coast of Iceland, are extremely interesting from a geological viewpoint.

The youngest of these islands, Surtsey, is barely forty years old. For the most part it was formed in a tephra eruption, but now the volcanic ash has solidified as palagonite. In this way Surtsey has

A bridge across Skjálfandafljót, one of Iceland's glacial rivers.

The Arctic Circle

acquired a secure rock foundation, but at the same time has deteriorated visibly from the attrition of the ocean and especially from the settling force of the bedrock. All this testifies to the interplay and formative power of the mighty forces which reign in the bowels of the earth and on its surface. The history of the formation of the landscape, and, in a nutshell, that of the whole earth, is obvious to those who look at Iceland with open eyes.

The greater part of the island consists of uninhabitable highlands, and in many places steep sea-cliffs extend out into the ocean. Glaciers cover approximately one-tenth of the surface, and an equivalent portion is covered with lava which flowed after the end of the Ice Age. The shoreline is indented with numerous bays, except on the south coast. There is an extensive lowland area in the south and west, but hardly any in the rest of the island, which is characterized by narrow strips of lowland along the coast and by valleys which extend from the bottoms of fjords up into the highland.

Weather

Iceland has a temperate maritime climate, with little protection against storms and winds. The summers are cool, and the winters relatively mild, owing to the presence of the Gulf Stream. There is considerable precipitation all year round and therefore many lakes and waterfalls; the widest and swiftest rivers are the ones which flow from glaciers. Bridges were not built across most of the major rivers until well into the twentieth century. The rivers always presented an obstacle to transport and affected the struggle for life of a sparse population in a harsh land.

Plant and Animal Life

Iceland's location near the arctic circle affects the flora and fauna. A closer look,

however, reveals many surprises, not least in the large number of life forms which flourish in Iceland. The chief explanation is perhaps the extent to which warm ocean currents counter-act the effects of the cold arctic air. Because of this the conditions for sustaining many species of birds in Iceland are better than in neighbouring countries, even those lying further south.

Vegetation

The plants growing in Iceland are typical of northern countries as well as of the mountainous areas of southern Europe. Many species which grow wild in Iceland are also common on the high slopes of the Alps, and most of the nearly five hundred plant species in Iceland are of European origin. There are, however, some noteworthy exceptions: the arctic river beauty and Lyngbye's sedge originate in North America.

The Icelandic plant community came into existence during the last ten thousand years, or after the end of the Ice Age, though scientists believe that some species survived from the last cold period of the Ice Age in mountainous areas which rose above the ice jacket, the so-called glacial skerries, from which they spread around the country at the end of the Ice Age. The Icelandic poppy is an example. As for trees, birch was the most common on the lowlands, with rowan and various species of willow growing amidst the birch. Birch forests covered all the dry ground to a height of four hundred metres above sea level, about one-fourth of the surface of the country.

The absence of forests today has a great effect on the appearance of the landscape. The settlement caused a great change in plant life, because in that harsh land men over-exploited the forests out of dire necessity. Lack of foresight and knowledge doubtlessly caused great damage as well. After eleven centuries of human habitation, only about one-hundredth of the land is clothed in forest. Other forms of vegetation have also been much changed as a result of both human activity and inclement nature. Volcanic eruptions have already been mentioned, and in addition it must not be overlooked that Iceland is extremely windy. Nonetheless there are fertile areas in many parts of the country where agriculture flourishes, especially the raising of sheep and the production of milk.

Deforestation has had diverse effects, the deterioration of the soil being the most serious. In many places, erosion has

Guillemot.

turned land which once was covered with vegetation into rocky wasteland. The soil is still being blown out to sea, and coming generations will have to come to grips with this problem. The main thing, however, is that Icelanders have come to understand the problem and are bent on reversing the process.

Birds

Birds occupy a large space in Icelandic nature. As with the plants, most birds are of European origin, but three species – the great northern diver, the harlequin duck and the Barrow's goldeneye – originate in North America. Well over seventy species breed in Iceland every year, and some four hundred species have been sighted in Iceland at least once. Most are vagrants which are seen only occasionally, and some are perennial winter guests or passage migrants. The puffin is by all accounts the most common breeding bird in Iceland. Several million couples breed around the entire coast, but the Westman Islands take pride in having the largest and densest colonies of puffins. The make-up of the breeding birds is different from that in neighbouring countries. As might be expected, sea-birds and waterfowl make up the overwhelming majority, and there are very few passerine species. Iceland is unusual in that breeding grounds are densely populated all across the island. The Mývatn area and a number of bird-cliffs are cases in point.

The sea and the extensive fertile shores provide nutrition for hordes of birds all the year round. The shores are especially important in the spring and autumn. In addition to the indigenous migrants, thousands of other birds stop on the shores during migration time. Iceland is an important stopping-off place for birds making the long journey between their breeding grounds north of the arctic circle and their winter homes in the south.

Blue whales and a whale watching boat from Húsavík.

Wild Mammals

Wild mammals are rather rare in Iceland, though they are more common in the surrounding ocean. The arctic fox seems to be the only animal which has lived in Iceland from the beginning, while other mammals were brought by humans in one way or another. The field mouse, for example, came with the early settlers, and rats came later on ships. Now and then, in years of dense pack ice, a polar bear will come ashore, but they have never become an established species. Some species have been brought in and either turned loose as wild animals or bred for the purpose of adding to the variety of farming. Reindeer were imported in the eighteenth century and turned loose in several places; they now roam only in the east of the country. In the first part of the twentieth century minks were imported, in order to breed them for their fur. Many escaped their confinement, and this eventually led to a wild stock of minks which has managed to gain a firm foothold in Icelandic nature. Because of the havoc they wreak on birdlife, they are not universally popular. Two species of seals make their home along the coast of Iceland, the grey seal and the harbour seal, both of which the Icelanders have used for sustenance through the centuries. Seals from Scandinavia occasionally turn up in Iceland, such as the bladdernose and the harp seal, and now and then there are sightings of walrus.

The sea around Iceland has long been known to be a busy area for whales, and for centuries whalers have sailed north to hunt them. An excess of hunting has caused the grey whale and the northern right whale to disappear entirely from Icelandic waters. On the other hand, some species are more plentiful around Iceland than anywhere else. The blue whale, the largest creature on earth, is frequently encountered off the west coast. On the average, around fifteen

other species of whale abound in nearby waters, and there are written records connecting over thirty species with Iceland. The most common species, such as the minke whale, the white-beaked dolphin and the porpoise, can often be seen just off the coast, and sometimes they come right up on the shore.

Fish

Over three hundred species of fish have been found in the waters around Iceland, only a tenth of which can be said to be of any significance for the national economy. In fact it is only a very few species – such as cod, herring and capelin – which form the basis of economic life. The annual Icelandic catch comes to nearly two million tons, of which capelin constitutes roughly one half. Cod, on the other hand, is by far the most important source of foreign revenue.

Approximately five species of fish are found in rivers and lakes, and indeed there is scarcely a creek without some hope of a catch. There are many abundant fishing rivers, including salmon-fishing rivers by the hundreds. Fishing in rivers and lakes has always played a key role in the struggle to stay alive in Iceland.

Other Animals

Insect life is quite meagre compared with neighbouring countries, as evidenced by the fact that ants, termites and native butterflies are not represented in Iceland. There are midges and black flies on the island, but surprisingly enough no mosquitoes, in contrast with other places around the earth at the same latitude. Iceland is also free of wild amphibians and reptiles.

THE PEOPLE

Icelandic society has come a long way in an amazingly short space of time. For centuries Icelanders sustained themselves by limited and primitive forms of employment, with little or no awareness of the industrial revolution and the technological advances which, among other things, led to the great urbanization of continental Europe during the nineteenth century. But in the course of the twentieth century Iceland leaped into the present, and almost by a single stroke a highly developed and technologically advanced society took the place of a stagnant rural society.

Icelandic towns and buildings have their own character, shaped by the fact that barely a century has passed since urban areas began to develop. Suitable building materials are not readily available on a volcanic island lacking forests. Beginning with the first settlers, human habitations were made of turf, wood and stone. A native Icelandic type of building evolved gradually, resulting in the passage farm and finally, around two centuries ago, the series of joined gabled buildings. The few turf buildings that still exist belong to district museums and are no longer inhabited.

It was not until poured concrete came into existence that endurable buildings were raised using native material. It is safe to say that eighty-five per cent or more of all the existing buildings in

Iceland were constructed after the end of World War II. An indication of the swift development of urban life is the fact that the capital city, Reykjavík, doubled its population in the last thirty to forty years.

One of the things that has characterized Icelandic architecture is the adapting of foreign ideas to Icelandic conditions. It was discovered, for example, that corrugated iron was more suitable than wood as an outer surface for houses in an inclement and changeable climate. Corrugated-iron houses, which characterize the older residential areas, are a good example of adaptation to local conditions. Icelandic architects have always turned to many different countries for their education and inspiration, which helps to account for the wide variety of buildings. Cases in point are the City Hall in the centre of Reykjavík and the swimming area at the Blue Lagoon, where modern construction is fitted into the surrounding lava.

The population of Iceland is barely three hundred thousand. It is by no means self-evident that such a sparse island population on the northern fringe of the world should be able to create a modern welfare society with one of the highest standards of living in the world. Public education is at a comparatively high level, and Icelanders have close ties with other countries. They are now in the forefront in the technologies of thermal heating, fisheries and fish processing. Intense efforts are being made to turn this technological expertise into a profitable export item, and Icelandic experts in these and other fields are spreading their knowledge more and more to distant corners of the world.

At the same time, Icelanders are thought to be tenacious of old and native values. The language and the history of the country and its people still play an important part in the minds of Icelanders, and it appears that a single, unified people has emerged from the centuries. The long distance between habitations in the old days was offset by considerable moving about and by frequent

Grenjaðarstaður in Suður-Þingeyjarsýsla. One of Iceland's old turf farms.

The Cathedral and House of Parliament in Reykjavík.

contacts between areas of the country, for example in search of work.

Government

From the earliest times, the form of government has been characterized by a strong central control, which was one of the factors helping to forge solidarity among the people. Shortly after the settlement, a general assembly was established, which was both a legislative and judicial assembly, made up of representatives from all parts of the country. The Alþing met first at Þingvellir in the year 930. Government was at first in the hands of native chieftains, until Iceland became subject to the Norwegian king soon after the middle of the thirteenth century.

From that time, and for more than six centuries, Iceland was under the control of foreign sovereigns, and it was during

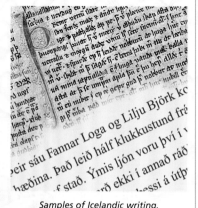

Samples of Icelandic writing, past and present.

this period that some of the greatest hardships in the history of Iceland were endured. But in spite of everything, it was not possible to erase from the consciousness of Icelanders the memory of their glorious past and their spirit of freedom.

Language

Icelandic is a Germanic language, more precisely a West-Nordic language. It is thought that from the very first centuries of settlement a single language was spoken, with very little in the way of dialect features, especially in comparison with neighbouring countries.

Because of the isolation of the country and the slow rate of progress there was relatively little change in the language. This explains how Icelanders today can read the medieval literature of the country without much difficulty. The Sagas of Icelanders are doubtless the best known works from the medieval period, and are considered to be Iceland's chief contribution to world literature.

The centuries-old, unbroken habit of writing in the native language gave it an invaluable foundation. The ability to read and write seems to have been common at all times. Book-publishing is unusually extensive and has had a great influence on the development of the language. Statistics reveal that more books per capita are published annually in Iceland than in any other country in the world. Of significance too is the fact that as early as the seventeenth century, learned men began to advocate a policy of language preservation. This policy came to maturity in the nineteenth century and is still very much alive today. It has been decisive in keeping the language strong in the face of foreign influences on Icelandic society. Previously there was considerable influence from Danish, while in recent decades the English language has made inroads, bringing many loan-words into Icelandic, especially slang words. The conservation policy has strong support among the people, and strenuous efforts are made to coin new words rather than giving a loose rein to borrowing from other languages.

As for the teaching of foreign languages, Danish was long in first position because of the centuries-old connection between Iceland and Denmark, but this has changed in recent years and English is now the first foreign language taught in schools. Most Icelanders find it comparatively easy to express themselves in at least one foreign language.

Wooden boats like this one have been replaced by large freezing trawlers.

Occupations

The settlers came to an untouched land, whose natural resources declined greatly as a result of over-use and ruthless exploitation over the centuries. Iceland is short on resources, with no valuable minerals like usable metals, coal or oil. Its inhabitants have always depended on the importation of various necessities. It was not until the beginning of the twentieth century that Iceland began to harness the energy of its waterfalls and the heat coming from the bowels of the earth. Today most houses derive their heat from thermal sources, and electricity is produced from water power. This produces an immense savings in foreign currency, not to mention the fact that very little pollution results from these sources of energy. These native energy sources are far from being exploited to the full, and in recent decades sales of energy to foreign industrial enterprises have increased significantly.

The Fishing Industry

Farming was Iceland's main occupation at first, and agricultural products were the main export items. But from the close of the Middle Ages products of the sea and fish processing have been the basis of the economy, and exports have

Fishing in Icelandic waters.

been rather one-sided. In fact, fluctuating prices in foreign fish markets have had an immense effect on the living conditions of a nation which has had to import many of its basic necessities, such as grain and various industrial goods. Fish was first dried for export, and "skreið" or dried fish is still an important export item, but nowadays frozen fish, salted fish, fish meal and cod liver oil are among the most important products.

With the aid of advanced technology and an increased understanding of the ecology of the sea, the fishing grounds are now exploited more rationally than before and without too much risk to the fishing stocks. The Icelandic fishing fleet is as highly developed as any in the world, but in spite of the increased fishing capacity an effort is being made to put a halt to ruthless exploitation. Most people are well aware that the fishing grounds are a renewable natural resource only as long as the stocks are preserved.

Industry

All around the country fish processing plants process the catches brought in by the fleet. There are also other kinds of food industry as well as light industry such as the manufacture of clothing. In recent decades many people have found work in construction projects, especially in the capital, Reykjavík, and its surroundings. Energy is being sold to heavy industries, such as aluminium plants, in an effort to provide a firmer basis for the national economy. In recent years there have been forward leaps in the fields of computer software and genetic research.

Agriculture

Icelandic agriculture has traditionally been based on livestock, but the importance of agricultural products in the export market has been decreasing. From early times, sheep have grazed freely in summer pastures all over the country. They are rounded up in the fall, and the lambs are taken to slaughter. At the present time lamb meat is consumed for the most part within the country and cattle are bred primarily for the production of dairy products for the internal market.

Iceland is home to a special breed of horse brought to the island by the first settlers. Icelandic horses are small, but they have a reputation for being good-natured and sure-footed. Horseback riding is a popular leisure activity in Iceland,

*Night at Laxárgljúfur.
The lights of one of Iceland's
hydroelectric powerplants can be seen
in the background.*

*Whale watching is a fast growing branch
of Iceland's tourist industry.*

*"Sólfar" (the Solar Ship), a sculpture
by the Icelandic artist Jón Gunnarsson,
on Reykjavík's waterfront.*

and breeding and riding Icelandic horses is becoming increasingly popular in other countries as well.

The portion of land under cultivation is around one-hundredth of the total surface and consists especially of acreage devoted to the production of animal fodder. Grain was once grown for human consumption, but this came to a stop at the end of the Middle Ages on account of the increasingly cold climate. In recent decades, however, the cultivation of grain for fodder has been on the increase. Iceland is able to produce enough potatoes for its own consumption, and other vegetables to some extent. What makes this possible is greenhouses in areas of thermal activity.

Tourism
Iceland is in the same position as many other countries in regard to tourism: there has been greater and swifter development in the tourist industry than in

*Rolls of hay. Only a small portion of
Iceland has been cultivated.*

other sectors of the economy. Now it has reached the point where the number of foreign tourists making their way to Iceland every year exceeds the total native population.

Culture and the Arts
In the twelfth, thirteenth and fourteenth centuries there was a great flourishing of literary activity in Iceland. Although we might expect that Icelanders, on the northern edge of the world, lived in isolation juring the Middle Ages, the literature testifies that the opposite was true. Those who wrote were well aware of the learned and creative writings of their time.

The Eddic poems were first written down in the thirteenth century after having been preserved for a long time in oral tradition. Their subject matter is an ancient inheritance from pagan times, and many of them are paralleled in the old poetry of other Germanic peoples. The names of the poets have long ago passed into oblivion, but nowhere has this poetry been better preserved than in Icelandic manuscripts. Skaldic poetry is another genre of old poetry; most skaldic poems are fitted into medieval sagas such as the Family Sagas and the Kings' Sagas.

The Family Sagas are regarded as the high point of saga literature, and for a long time they have helped to shape the self-image of the Icelandic people. They describe the origin of the nation and the reasons for settling in Iceland. Some of the best-known are *Njal's Saga, Egil's Saga* and *Laxdæla Saga*.

Other well-known works include the *Book of Icelanders* and the *Book of Settlements*, which describe the settle-

ment from the very beginning, and sagas of foreign potentates, especially the kings of Norway. Sagas of bishops from the Catholic period were also written, and other sagas which describe the struggle for power among the leading families. Everywhere behind these narratives the life of the Icelanders at that time can be discerned.

The best-known writer of medieval sagas in Scandinavia is, without doubt, Snorri Sturluson (1179–1241). He wrote the *Snorra Edda,* a handbook on the art of writing poetry; *the Saga of St. Olaf,* king of Norway; and *Heimskringla,* a compilation of the lives of many Norwegian kings.

Halldór Laxness (1902–1998) is the best-known writer in the modern period. He was particularly productive as a writer of novels, but he also expressed himself in other literary forms and took an active part in debates on national issues of the time. Halldór Laxness was awarded the Nobel Prize for Literature in 1955, the highest international recognition that has ever been given to an Icelandic writer.

Icelanders have been less productive, on the international scale, in the other arts, though there was a special native tradition of wood-carving, especially of household items and utensils for everyday use. One of the most remarkable products of the special Icelandic tradition of wood-carving is the formation of the letters of the Roman alphabet by skilled carvers, the so-called "höfðaletur".

Some scholars have proposed that the ancient Icelandic song melodies or "stemmur" are remnants of the oldest and earliest folk songs in Europe.

The art of music finally took a great leap forward at the beginning of the twentieth century when the long isolation

*Kristján Kristjánsson and Ellen
Kristjánsdóttir. Musical life in Iceland
is flourishing as never before.*

was broken, and musical life is now flourishing as never before. Icelandic musicians are active in a variety of musical forms, and public support is strong. There is a symphony orchestra, not to mention an untold number of chamber music groups and other performers of classical music. The fame of Icelandic pop musicians has also extended abroad. Most people are familiar with the singer Björk and the group Sigur Rós.

Painting has also developed swiftly, and Icelanders are more and more involved in all branches of the modern arts, for example film-making.

USEFUL INFORMATION

GETTING TO ICELAND

• By air: There are regularly scheduled flights between Iceland and the mainland of Europe, as well as the east coast of the United States, all year round. In the summer there is additional service to more places abroad, and flights are more frequent. Apart from scheduled flights, charter flights between Iceland and continental Europe are available during the summer.

• By ship: There are no passenger ships sailing between Iceland and other countries, but freighters with regularly scheduled sailings have cabins intended for passengers. During the summer there is weekly ferry service between Iceland, the Faroes, Denmark and Norway, transporting both passengers and automobiles.

TRANSPORTATION WITHIN ICELAND

• By air: There is regular passenger service all year round between the capital, Reykjavík, and other parts of the country. In addition, companies in many areas of the country offer rental and sight-seeing flights.

• By ship: In some places there are regularly scheduled ferries, transporting both passengers and cars. The ferries are a part of the national highway system, and they sail almost every day of the year. Tourists also have a wide selection of sightseeing sailings.

• By scheduled busses: Regularly scheduled bus service is available all over the country all year round, with additional service to the highlands and uninhabited parts of the country during the summer. Tickets are available either at bus stations or directly from the driver. A significant discount is offered for certain types of tickets, such as for 1–2–3–4 week periods. Discounts are also available for certain parts of the highway system, for example Route No. 1 ("the ring road") or the highland routes. Busses for group tours can be hired for long or short trips, with or without a guide.

**• By rented or private car,
or by motorcycle or bicycle:** Many car rental agencies, all around the country, offer automobiles of various types, from small passenger cars to powerful vehicles with four-wheel drive. In recent years there has been an increase in the number of tourists choosing to travel on their own, and a considerable number of people on holiday trips bring their own cars. In addition, an untold number choose to travel around on motorcycles or bicycles.

• Travelling on Icelandic roads: The national highway system covers 8,500 kilometres, including an uninterrupted road all the way around the country, Route No. 1, known as "the ring road". Not all roads have yet been paved with a permanent surface. Gravel roads are common, of varying quality and passability depending on the time of year and the weather.

In the summer, however, Icelandic roads are generally usable by all kinds of cars. Drivers are advised to be careful of the loose gravel on the surface of unpaved roads, and especially on the edges. In addition, the gravel roads tend to be narrow and winding and thus not suitable for fast driving. Drivers must always take special caution, for example when meeting or passing other cars.

It must be kept in mind that the roads in uninhabited areas are only open in high summer, and as a rule not for normal passenger cars. Highland trips can also have other hazards. All sorts of weather can occur, and even in the summer the temperature might go below freezing, accompanied by snow or sleet. In order for journeys into the uninhabited areas to be safe and pleasurable, travellers must plan their equipment carefully, anticipating every eventuality. Information about the condition of the roads is available in information centres and petrol stations around the country.

The maximum legal driving speed is variable, all the way from 30 kilometres an hour in some settled areas to 90 kilometres an hour on surfaced highways. Driving is on the right-hand side of the road, and headlights must be lit twenty-four hours a day all year long.

• Health care and insurance: The Icelandic health care system is among the best in the world, staffed with highly educated physicians and nurses. There are medical clinics in every urban area, and in Reykjavík and other large towns there is round-the-clock emergency service. When an accident or emergency occurs, the nearest police station can be reached by dialling the emergency number **112** almost everywhere in the country, and from there all

Drivers must always take special caution on Icelandic roads.

Land Surface:	103.000 km²
Covered with vegetation	19,5%
Cultivated	1%
Lakes	3%
Glaciers	11.5%
Lava	10.5%
Sand	4%
Barren	50.5%
Territorial waters*	758,000 km²

*within 200 miles

Temperature and Precipitation, 1961–1990

Temperature in Celsius (ºC)

Reykjavík:					
Average:	Jan. −0.5	July	+10.6	Annual	+4.3
Highest:	Jan. +9.9	July	+24.3		+24.3
Lowest:	Jan. −19.7	July	+1.4		−19.7
Precipitation (mm):	Jan. 76	July	52	Annual	799

Akureyri:					
Average:	Jan. −2.2	July	+10.5	Annual	+3.2
Highest:	Jan. +13.0	July	+27.6		+29.4
Lowest:	Jan. −21.6	July	+1.3		−23.0
Precipitation (mm):	Jan. 55	July	33	Annual	490

necessary measures will be taken at once to ensure that help arrives as quickly as possible. Pharmacies are available in all parts of the country; in Reykjavík and other large towns, some are open twenty-four hours a day.

• Luggage and clothing: The weather is variable, and the unexpected can occur at all times of the year. It is therefore important when travelling to be ready for all contingencies and to secure the appropriate equipment. Warm and protective clothing is absolutely necessary: warm underwear, woollen socks and sweater, windproof outer-wear and head covering, rain gear, rubber boots and hiking boots – to mention only a few items. Those journeying into the highlands need to make appropriate preparations, including a warm sleeping bag. Swimming gear is likely to be used nearly everywhere. Owing to Iceland's unusual access to and use of thermal sources of heat, indoor and outdoor swimming pools are available in all settled areas, and warmwater creeks and pools are to be found off the beaten track in many parts of the country.

• Maps and handbooks: Survey maps, road maps and travel books in many languages are available in bookshops, information offices and petrol stations around the country.

• Currency: The native currency is called the "króna", consisting of a hundred "aurar". Nearly all types of foreign currency can be exchanged in banks and hotels around the country, and some shops even accept payment in foreign currency. All kinds of goods and services may be obtained by using credit cards.

• Shopping, duty-free goods and refunds of the value added tax: The selection of consumer goods in the shops, including clothing and fashion items from world-famous brands, is very good. As for Icelandic products, hand-made art objects and woolen goods are popular, as well as top-grade food items: lamb meat, all kinds of seafood, smoked and pickled salmon and so forth. The VAT can be refunded (as much as 15% of the sales price) on leaving the country as long as the purchase reaches a certain minimum amount and no more than thirty days have elapsed from the date of purchase. In addition, the duty-free shops at the Keflavík airport offer a rich selection of duty-free goods.

• Post and telephone: The country is linked by

an automatic telephone system, and there are telephone stations and post offices in every settled area. Coin-operated machines are available everywhere, and in almost all parts of the country it is possible to reach the whole world from cell phones.

• **Lodgings:** Hotels are available on all levels, for those who want to enjoy maximum luxury as well as for those who simply want a decent place to stay without risk to their budgets. In many urban areas, especially Reykjavík, the space available in guest-houses and in private homes has increased greatly in recent years. The same may be said for farmhouse lodgings all over the country. Almost without exception, these lodgings are clean and neat, with access to good plumbing and also to a kitchen for those who wish to. Youth hostels exist in the larger urban areas, and in the uninhabited areas there are mountain huts where guests can stay – provided they have brought their sleeping bags.

• **Restaurants and outdoor activities:** Although there are a number of restaurants which offer luxurious menus and lavish surroundings, more reasonably priced restaurants are in the majority. Many of these make special offers in an attempt to meet the needs of foreign tourists.

There has been a large increase in the number of tourists who regard their holiday travel as a chance to enjoy the outdoors and healthy exercise, who prefer creating their own activities to relaxing passively. Iceland is well suited for travellers who long for active participation of this kind. There are many possibilities: sight-seeing trips by land or sea or sky, white-water rafting, jeep and motor-sled trips across the glaciers. In addition there are golfing, walking and horseback trips, not to mention unforgettable bird- and whale-watching or fishing in rivers or lakes or the sea.

• **Icelandic names:** The Icelandic system for personal names never fails to interest and surprise foreigners. Most persons use their baptismal name (first name) rather than their last name. The "last name" is based on the baptismal name of the father (most commonly) or the mother (rarely). The name of the parent occurs in the possessive form, followed by "-son" or "dóttir" (son or daughter). It is customary for the same baptismal name to recur again and again in the same family. The names of most Icelanders are formed in this way, although there are also a few family names.

Icelanders never use the last name by itself, and they commonly make do with just the baptismal name. There is much less emphasis on the last name than in other countries. In public records, such as the telephone book, people are listed by their baptismal names (first names), not by their last names.

• **Spelling:** "Accent marks" over letters (vowels) do not indicate accent or length, but rather a different sound from the same letter without a mark over it. The letters Þ/þ (pronounced like unvoiced "th") and Ð/ð (pronounced like voiced "th") appear unusual, but they have been used in Icelandic writing from ancient times. Both of these letters were adopted from Old English

handwriting; the letter "Þ" also occurred in runic writings, which Norsemen used before they adopted the Latin alphabet.

ℹ TOURIST INFORMATION CENTRES

Reykjavík
Bankastræti 2 • 101 Reykjavík • tel.: 562 3045
fax: 562 3057 • tourinfo@tourinfo.is

Hafnarfjörður
Vesturgata 8 • 220 Hafnarfjörður • tel.: 565 0661
fax: 565 2914 • tourist-info@lava.is

Grindavík
Víkurbraut 62 • 240 Grindavík • tel.: 420 1109
fax: 420 1111 • tourinfo@grindavik.is

Keflavík
Hafnargata 57 • Kjarni • 230 Keflavík
tel.: 421 6760 • fax: 421 6199 • rtb@rnb.is

Akranes
Kirkjubraut 3 • 300 Akranes • tel.: 431 3327
fax: 431 4327 • info@akranes.is

Borgarnes
Brúartorg 4–6 • 310 Borgarnes • tel.: 437 2214
fax: 437 2314 • tourinfo@vesturland.is

Snæfellsbær/Ólafsvík
Gamla pakkhúsið • 355 Ólafsvík • tel.: 436 1543

Stykkishólmur
Borgarbraut 4 • 340 Stykkishólmur
tel.: 438 1150, fax: 438 1780 • efling@islandia.is

Ísafjörður
Aðalstræti 7 • 400 Ísafjörður • tel.: 456 5121
fax: 456 5122

Hrútarfjörður
Staðarskáli • 500 Staður • tel.: 451 1150
fax: 451 1107 • stadur@if.is

Blönduós
Brautarhvammur • 540 Blönduós
tel.: 452 4520 • fax: 452 4063
ferdhun@isholf.is

Varmahlíð
560 Varmahlíð • tel.: 453 8860
upplvarm@krokur.is

Siglufjörður
Suðurgata 6 • 580 Siglufjörður • tel.: 467 1950
fax: 467 1952

Akureyri
Hafnarstræti 82 • 600 Akureyri • tel.: 462 773
fax: 461 3303 • tourinfo@est.is

Húsavík
The Husavik Whale Centre • 640 Húsavík
tel.: 464 2520, icewhale@centrum.is

Mývatn
Reykjahlíðarskóli • 660 Mývatn • tel.: 464 4390
fax: 464 4378 • myvatn.info@ismennt.is

Jökulsárgljúfur National Park
671 Kópasker • tel.: 465 2195 • fax: 465 2359,
gljufur@isholf.is

Egilsstaðir
Kaupvangur 6 • 700 Egilsstaðir • tel.: 471 2320
fax: 471 1863 • east@east.is

Seyðisfjörður
Ránargata 6 • 710 Seyðisfjörður • tel.: 472 1551
fax: 472 1315 • ferdamenning@sfk.is

Hornafjörður
Hafnarbraut 25 • 780 Hornafjörður
tel.: 478 1500 • markadsrad@southeast.is

Skaftafell National Park
785 Fagurhólsmýri • tel.: 478 1627
fax: 478 1627 • skaftafell@natturuvernd.is

Information Centre at Skaftárbrú
880 Kirkjubæjarklaustur • tel.: 487 4620
fax: 487 4842 • skaftinfo@isgatt.is

Vík
Víkurbraut 28 • 870 Vík • tel.: 487 1509
vik@hotmail.com

Hvolsvöllur
860 Hvolsvöllur • tel.: 487 8781
fax: 487 8782, njala@islandia.is

Hveragerði
Breiðamörk 2 • 810 Hveragerði • tel.: 483 4601
fax: 483 4604 • tourinfo@hveragerdi.is

Westman Islands/Vestmannaeyjar
Vestmannabraut 38 • 900 Vestmannaeyjar
tel.: 481 3555 • fax: 481 1572 • slorn@isholf.is

Iceland Tourist Board website: www.icelandtouristboard.com

Wonders of Iceland
© 2002 JPV Publishers
Author: Helgi Guðmundsson
Translation: Robert Cook
Foreword: Vigdís Finnbogadóttir
Designer and creative editor: Jón Ásgeir í Aðaldal
Printed by: Oddi hf.

JPV PUBLISHERS · Reykjavík · 2002

ISBN: 9979-761-67-9

Picture Credits

(t = top; tl = top left; tc = top centre; tr = top right;
b = bottom; bl = bottom left; bc = bottom centre;
br = bottom right)

Brooks Walker: 28, 52, 53; Friðþjófur Helgason: 60 br;
Heimir Harðarson: 59 tl, 61 tc; Jóhann Óli Hilmarsson:
8, 12, 17, 22, 27, 30, 37, 38, 40, 43, 58 tr, 61 tr;
Jóhann Ísberg: Cover (front), 9, 10, 11, 13, 14, 15, 16, 19,
23, 24, 25, 26, 41, 46, 47, 48, 49, 54, 55, 59 br, 60 tl,
61 br; Jón Ásgeir: 7, 29, 42, 51, 58 bl, 59 bl, 60 tr,
61 tl, bl, 62; Ólafur K. Magnússon: 57 tr; Sigurður H.
Stefnisson: Cover (back), 18, 20, 21, 31, 32, 33, 34, 35,
36, 39, 44, 45, 50

More pictures by Brooks Walker, Friðþjófur Helgason,
Heimir Harðarson, Jóhann Ísberg and Sigurður H.
Stefnisson can be seen at: www.myndabanki.is